Grassland Food Chains

Louise and Richard Spilsbury

H www.heinemann.co.uk/library
Visit our website to find out more information about Heinemann Library books.

To order:
☎ Phone 44 (0) 1865 888066
🗎 Send a fax to 44 (0) 1865 314091
💻 Visit the Heinemann Bookshop at www.heinemann.co.uk/library to browse our catalogue and order online.

First published in Great Britain by Heinemann Library, Halley Court, Jordan Hill, Oxford OX2 8EJ, part of Harcourt Education. Heinemann is a registered trademark of Harcourt Education Ltd.

Editorial: Sarah Eason and Kathy Peltan
Design: Jo Hinton-Malivoire and AMR
Illustration: Words and Publications
Picture Research: Ruth Blair
Production: Camilla Smith

Originated by Ambassador Litho Ltd
Printed in China by WKT Company Limited.

The paper used to print this book comes from sustainable resources.

ISBN 0 431 11905 8
09 08 07 06 05
10 9 8 7 6 5 4 3 2 1

British Library Cataloguing in Publication Data
Spilsbury, Louise and Richard
Food Chains: Grasslands
577.4'16

A full catalogue record for this book is available from the British Library.

Acknowledgements
The Publishers would like to thank the following for permission to reproduce photographs:
Alamy p. **14**; Corbis pp. **5** (Paul A. Souders), **7** (William Manning), **8** (Joe McDonald), **10** (Craig Lovell), **11** (Galen Rowell), **12**, **27** (RF), **13** (Lynda Richardson), **16** (Yann Arthus-Bertrand), **17** (Tony Wharton/Frank Lane Picture Agency), **23** (Darrell Gulin), **24** (Wolfgang Kaehler), **26** (Patrick Robert), p. **25**; NHPA pp. **15** (Ann and Steve Toon), **18** (Stephen Dalton), **22** (Martin Harvey).

Cover photograph of a cheetah chasing a young gazelle reproduced with permission of NHPA/Christophe Ratier.

The Publishers would like to thank Michael Scott for his assistance in the preparation of this book.

Contents

Words written in bold, **like this**, are explained in the Glossary.

What is a grassland food web?

Plants, animals and other living things rely on each other for life. This is because all **organisms** eat and are eaten by other organisms. For example, in a grassland **habitat** crickets eat grass and are eaten by mice. When living things die and rot other organisms, such as insects, eat them. If you draw lines between each of the organisms that eat each other, you create a diagram called a food web. It is called a web because it looks like a very tangled spider's web! The arrows lead from the food to the animal that eats it.

This food web is from pampas grassland in Argentina.

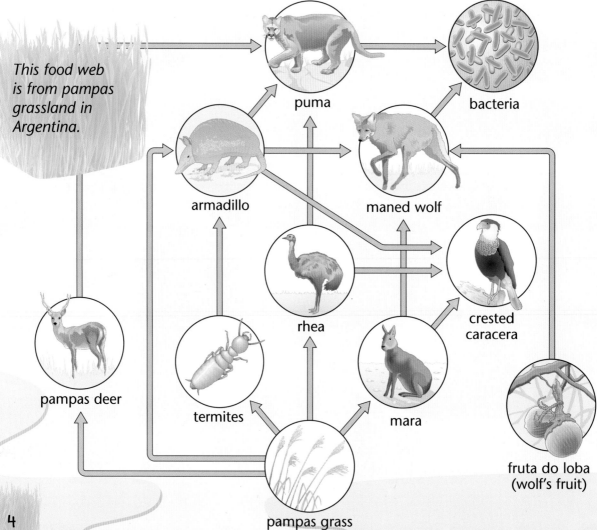

puma

bacteria

armadillo

maned wolf

rhea

crested caracera

pampas deer

termites

mara

fruta do loba
(wolf's fruit)

pampas grass

What are grassland habitats like?

Grasslands are large open spaces where the soil is too poor or the weather too dry for trees and many other plants to grow. Instead, tough wild grasses take over the land. Other grasslands were made by people when they cleared forests. Farm animals, such as sheep and cows, stop the forest coming back by eating plants before they can grow tall.

Tropical grasslands are called savannahs. These grasslands are hot all year, and only get short bursts of rain. Savannahs have scattered trees and shrubs as well as grasses. Some grasslands grow in **temperate** areas that have hot summers and cold winters. These have fewer trees than the savannah. They are called prairies in America, pampas in Argentina and steppes in Asia.

The tall grasses of the African savannah provide cover for hunters, such as this cheetah.

What is a grassland food chain?

Food webs look quite complicated, but they are made up of a series of simple interlocking food chains. Food chains show the **organisms** that eat each other as links in a single chain. They follow the movement of **nutrients** and **energy** as it passes from one link to another.

Most living things are part of more than one food chain because they eat or are eaten by more than one kind of organism. This makes them part of a more complex food web, which is safer for the organisms within it. If an animal relied on only one food source and that food supply ran out, the animal would starve.

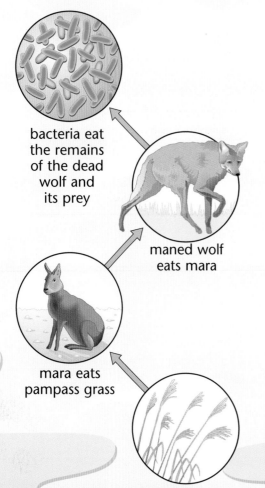

bacteria eat the remains of the dead wolf and its prey

maned wolf eats mara

mara eats pampass grass

pampas grass

This is a diagram of a grassland food chain. The arrows show which way the energy moves. Some energy is lost as it passes from one link in the chain to the next.

In the American prairies, flowers such as these goldenrods and purple prairie blazing stars grow among the grasses.

Starting the chain

The Sun is the source of energy for all organisms in the world. Most food chains start with plants because they can trap some of the energy in sunlight in their leaves. They use it to make food in a process called **photosynthesis**. These foods, along with nutrients taken up through their roots, allow plants to grow and make new plants.

Animals cannot make their own food – some get the energy and nutrients they need by eating plant parts. In grassland **habitats**, bees and butterflies feed on **nectar** from flowers, while caterpillars, beetles and grasshoppers munch leaves. Other animals get energy by eating plant-eaters or other meat-eaters. This is how energy flows through the food chain and through the habitat.

Making the chain

Food chains usually start with a plant **producer**. Plants are called producers because they make (produce) food. Animals have to consume (eat) other organisms to get the energy they need, so they are called **consumers**.

Animals that eat only plants are known as **herbivores**. In food chains herbivores are called **primary consumers**, because they eat the producers. **Carnivores** are animals that eat other animals, such as snakes. They are known as **secondary consumers**. Secondary consumers eat both primary consumers (the herbivores) and other secondary consumers. Animals that eat both plants and other animals are called **omnivores**. They are primary and secondary consumers.

Copperhead snakes are carnivores, or secondary consumers. This one is eating a deer mouse.

There are always more producers than primary consumers in food chains, and more primary consumers than secondary consumers.

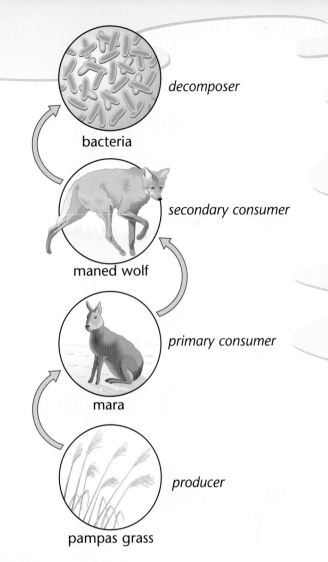

decomposer

bacteria

secondary consumer

maned wolf

primary consumer

mara

producer

pampas grass

More links in the chain

When plants and animals die, other organisms can still use the energy stored in their bodies. **Scavengers** eat the dead remains of other animals. Jackals and white-backed vultures are two grassland scavengers. **Decomposers** such as **bacteria** and **fungi** feed on any dead remains not taken by scavengers. Decomposers break down the remains into tiny pieces. They eat some of them and some get washed into the soil. Plants take in these soil nutrients through their roots, and so the food chain begins again.

Without decomposers the other organisms in a habitat would eventually die out. Only decomposers can break down dead organisms and their waste into a form that plant producers can use to create new supplies of energy.

Breaking the chain

If some organisms in a food web die out, it can be disastrous for other organisms in the web. Sometimes natural events can break the links in a food chain. Fire is a major part of grassland life. It can destroy all the grass, shrubs and trees in an area very quickly. The animals that usually eat the plants may starve and die. This means the carnivores that eat those animals will have less food to eat, too.

These vulture scavengers are feeding on the body of a dead zebra in Tanzania, Africa.

Which producers live in grasslands?

Grasses are the main **producers** in grassland food chains, but trees are also important producers in savannah **habitats**.

Grasses

There are different kinds of grasses in different grassland habitats, such as pampas grass in the Argentinean pampas and feather grass on the Asian steppe, but they all share similar features. The feature that makes them so successful is their ability to live through long periods without rain. This is why grasses are found all over the world. Grasses grow quickly and soon produce seeds. Grass plants are **pollinated** and their seeds are carried by the wind, so they spread over a wide area. In some grasslands, colourful wild flowers grow among the grasses.

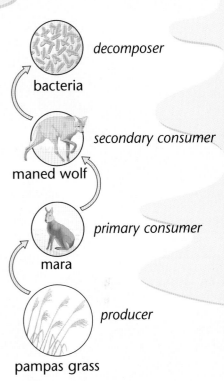

decomposer
bacteria

secondary consumer
maned wolf

primary consumer
mara

producer
pampas grass

On the flat plains of Montana, USA, grasses dotted with flowers cover the land.

Tropical grassland trees

Tropical grassland trees are **adapted** (suited) to survive the dry, hot **climate**. Many lose their leaves in the dry season, and burst into life in the wet season. Some, such as euphorbias and acacias, store water in their tough stems. To stop animals eating their leaves and shoots, acacia trees have thorns. Some euphorbias contain a bad-tasting milky **sap** that puts off most hungry animals!

These acacias are the most common trees in the African savannah.

Breaking the chain: producers

In parts of the North American prairie the **larvae** of monarch butterflies feed on milkweed leaves that are poisonous to most insects. The build-up of poison in the larvae and later the adult makes the butterflies poisonous and protects them from being eaten by birds. To farmers milkweed is a weed. When they burn or cut down these plants, many monarch butterflies die too.

Which primary consumers live in grasslands?

Insects are the main **primary consumers** in many grasslands. Lots of crickets, locusts, grasshoppers, and many kinds of beetles eat parts of plants. Although insect jaws are small they are strong and can bite through leaves, stems and seeds. Grassland insects use wings to fly or long legs to jump from plant to plant to find a meal.

Other small grassland animals

Many birds also eat parts of plants. Prairie chickens feed on leaves, fruit and seeds. Many small grassland **herbivores** live in underground burrows safe from **predators** and fires. On prairies, prairie dogs eat plant seeds, roots, leaves, flowers and fruits. Gophers and mole rats dig tunnels to eat roots and other underground plant parts. The long-legged and large-eared jackrabbit **grazes** on grass.

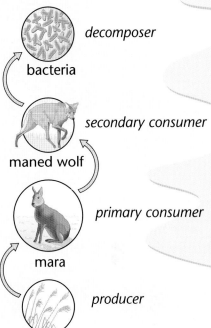

decomposer
bacteria

secondary consumer
maned wolf

primary consumer
mara

producer
pampas grass

Birds such as this American goldfinch feed on the seeds of grassland flowers.

Large grassland herbivores

There are many large grassland herbivores. These primary consumers usually live and feed in herds, so that some members of the group can look out for predators. Some, such as bison and antelopes, have extra stomach chambers that help them digest tough, chewy grasses more thoroughly. Others, like zebras and white rhinos, do not have these. They have to eat even more grass to get enough **nutrients** from it to survive.

In **tropical** grasslands some large herbivores also eat tree parts. Giraffes and black rhino eat leaves, buds and fruit from acacia trees. They use long tongues to snatch leaves from among the thorns of acacias. Elephants strip bark from trees with their trunks, or push them over to eat their leaves and fruit. They pass the food from their trunk into their mouth.

This giraffe is eating from an acacia tree in Kenya, Africa.

Which secondary consumers live in grasslands?

Carnivores, **omnivores** and **scavengers** are all **secondary consumers**. Grassland secondary consumers have a variety of ways to find their food. Snakes such as puff adders have little pits on their head that are sensitive to heat. These help them to catch warm-bodied **rodents** at night. Nile crocodiles lie in wait at some grassland waterholes, ready to catch **grazers** that come to drink there.

Bird life

Many grassland birds are also secondary consumers. The red-billed oxpecker hitches a ride on the backs of large grazing animals such as buffalo. It eats **parasites** called ticks that bite through the **herbivore's** skin and feed on their blood. **Birds of prey** such as the steppe eagle fly over grassland waiting for animals such as hamsters and voles to emerge from their burrows.

decomposer
bacteria

secondary consumer
maned wolf

primary consumer
mara

producer
pampas grass

Secretary birds often hunt snakes and lizards, but this one has caught a rodent.

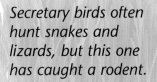

15

Dogs, cats and scavengers

Grassland dogs include African wild dogs, maned wolves and dingoes. They eat **prey** such as rodents, rabbits, antelope and zebra. On the savannah lions, leopards and cheetahs hunt for food. A large animal such as an antelope can provide them with enough food for several days. Grassland scavengers include birds such as vultures and marabou storks, and animals such as brown hyenas. Hyenas sometimes chase off lions from their kills.

Lions work in teams to bring down prey larger than themselves.

Breaking the chain: secondary consumers

On the American prairie farmers once poisoned prairie dogs because they mistakenly believed that their burrows were a hazard for cattle and that they competed with cattle for grass. Poisoning and shooting reduced prairie dog populations by 90 per cent and made the black-footed ferret, which eats prairie dogs, an **endangered species**.

Which decomposers live in grasslands?

Grassland **decomposers** include **bacteria** and **fungi**. They live in the soil in open grasslands, because dead animals and plants and their waste usually end up there.

Bacteria and fungi

Bacteria and fungi break down a great deal of dead matter and waste in grassland **habitats**. They cannot 'eat' food as animals do. They feed by releasing chemicals called enzymes into the dead animal or plant. The enzymes break down the dead body into liquid **nutrients**. Bacteria or fungi then absorb some of these nutrients to feed. The rest washes into the ground, making a rich soil for grasses and other plants to grow in.

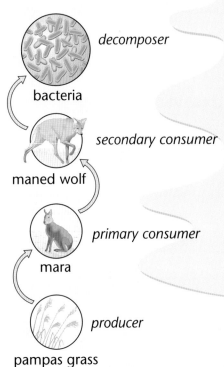

decomposer

bacteria

secondary consumer

maned wolf

primary consumer

mara

producer

pampas grass

Mushrooms and toadstools are the reproductive parts of a fungus, which produce tiny, seed-like spores. The main part of the fungus is a network of tiny threads that run through the soil.

Animals that help decomposers

When some animals eat dead **organisms**, they help break them down into smaller bits that decomposers can use. These mini-**scavengers** include insects and worms.

Termites are ant-like insects that live in groups in earth nests up to 10 metres (almost 33 feet) high. They feed mainly on dead wood and plants. This is useful because plants contain cellulose, a substance that it is hard for any other insects to break down.

The small, flat carrion beetle finds **carrion** (dead animals) by smell. It buries the bodies of small animals and lays eggs on them. When the **larvae** hatch out of the eggs they can feed on the body.

Grassland soil contains millions of microscopic worms called nematodes. Some are **parasites** on plants, but most are beneficial to the soil. They feed on bacteria, fungi or other nematodes, and **excrete** nutrients into the soil.

The maggots that feed on dead animals are the larvae of flies. Adult flies lay their eggs in a dead animal and the larvae that hatch out feed on its flesh.

How are grassland food chains different in different places?

Food chains and webs can be very different from one grassland to another. These are three important grasslands.

The African savannah

The biggest **tropical** grassland in the world is the savannah, which stretches from southern Africa up to the Sahara desert in the north. As well as the patches of grass that grow here, there are areas of thorny bushes and open woodland.

Grasses here provide food for vast herds of wildebeest and zebra. Giraffe feed on the tallest acacia trees and black rhinos nibble smaller bushes. African wild dogs hunt in large groups to bring down large **herbivores** such as wildebeest. Lions hide in the grass as they creep up on their **prey**. Other smaller savannah **primary consumers** include insects, which are eaten by **secondary consumers** such as lizards and meerkats.

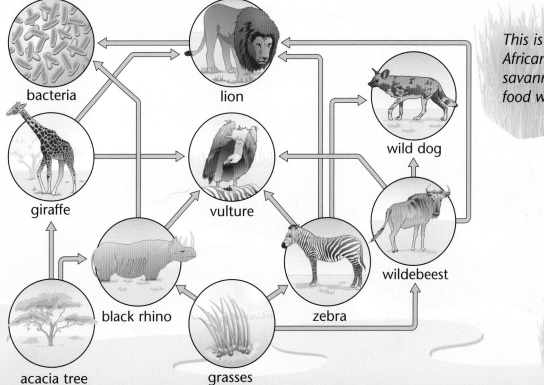

bacteria

lion

giraffe

vulture

wild dog

black rhino

zebra

wildebeest

acacia tree

grasses

This is an African savannah food web.

The American prairie

Prairie once covered the flat land in the middle of North America from Canada down to Texas. Much of this area is now farmland. The main prairie **producers** are grasses. Big bluestem is one of the tallest at up to 3 metres (nearly 10 feet) high. The grasses are eaten by grasshoppers, prairie dogs and bison. Bison are up to 2 metres (6.5 feet) tall and eat 30 kilograms (66 pounds) of plants each day!

Western meadowlark, prairie chickens and skink eat insects such as grasshoppers. Rattlesnakes eat a varied diet including lizards, frogs, **rodents**, birds' eggs, chicks and prairie dogs. Coyotes **scavenge** large animal remains or hunt small prey such as prairie dogs. Prairie ants carry seeds and insects back to underground nests to eat.

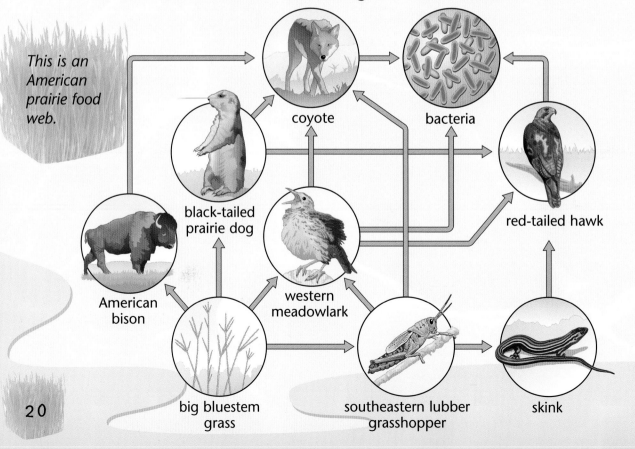

This is an American prairie food web.

coyote

bacteria

black-tailed prairie dog

red-tailed hawk

American bison

western meadowlark

big bluestem grass

southeastern lubber grasshopper

skink

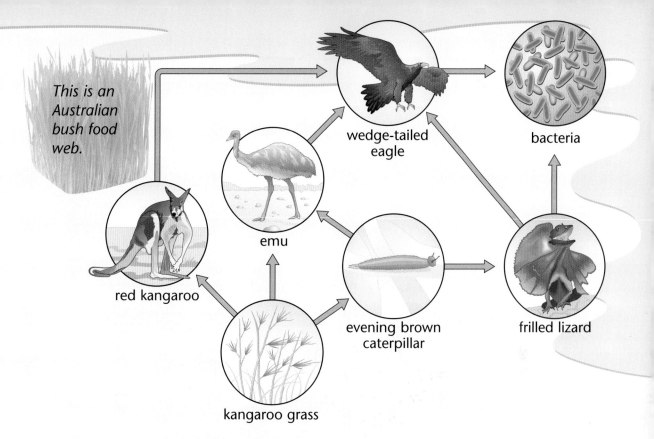

This is an Australian bush food web.

wedge-tailed eagle

bacteria

emu

red kangaroo

evening brown caterpillar

frilled lizard

kangaroo grass

The Australian bush

Bush extends across northern and parts of southern Australia. It is a type of dry savannah grassland dotted with trees. Gum or eucalyptus trees are typical bush trees. Koalas are one of the few herbivores that can eat the oily leaves of these trees, as they have special **bacteria** in their stomachs to help them digest this food. Some of the largest Australian animals such as kangaroos and wallabies **graze** on low plants such as kangaroo grass.

The emu is a bird that is about 1.5 metres tall (almost 5 feet) and that cannot fly. It eats plants but is also a secondary consumer of insects. The wedge-tailed eagle is a **bird of prey** that hunts striped emu chicks hidden amongst the bush grasses, and **mammals** such as kangaroos. The eagle is also the major bush scavenger.

What happens to a food web when a food chain breaks down?

The food chains and webs in many **habitats** are under threat because of human activities. When something affects one link in a food chain, it can have disastrous effects for the chain and other parts of the food web.

Overgrazing

Some grasslands are damaged when too many animals are allowed to **graze** an area. The grass plants get tugged up by their roots so they cannot regrow. This is called overgrazing. Once the blanket of grass that covered the land is gone, the fertile top layer of soil blows away or is washed away by rain. This leaves very dry land where little grows. Overgrazing by wild and farm animals has destroyed many of the grasslands in the world, sometimes even turning them into deserts.

Overgrazing in this part of India has turned what was once grassland into dusty desert.

Habitat destruction

Many wild grassland habitats have disappeared. Huge areas have been converted to crop-growing farmland. Some areas have been taken over by people for building houses, offices or factories. Others have been taken for parks, playing fields or golf courses.

Wild prairie grassland once covered a huge area of North America. Since the beginning of the 20th century most of this land has been ploughed up to grow another kind of grass – wheat. As more and more of the wild prairie has been lost to farming, more and more grazing animals have died out in the area, including herds of pronghorns (a type of antelope). This means that their **predators** further along the food chain, such as wolves, have also disappeared from these areas.

*In Africa elephants are an **endangered species** because people hunt them for their ivory tusks.*

Hunting

People hunt and kill grassland animals for many reasons. For example, African rhinos are hunted just for their valuable horns. On American prairies in the past, bison were hunted almost to **extinction** for their meat and skins. In the Australian bush today, thousands of kangaroos are killed each year for their skins, which are often used to make football boots.

Breaking the chain: unwanted additions

When a new link is introduced to food webs it can be disastrous. For example, in the mid-1800s people took wild rabbits to Australia from England for sport hunting. They spread rapidly and became one of the worst pests in the Australian bush. Rabbits eat so many of the grasses and other plants that they leave little food and shelter for **native** animals. By removing so many plants they also damage the soil.

How can we protect grassland food chains?

Around the world, scientists and **conservation** workers are working to protect the living things in grassland food chains and webs.

Scientists at work

Scientists study **endangered species** of plants and animals to understand how they live, how they fit into grassland food chains and webs, and what they need to survive. For example, in the African savannah people track rare black rhinos by recognizing and following their footprints. They work out what area the rhinos roam over to find the food plants they need. They study how the rhino population changes over time and whether illegal hunting is going on. The scientists can then make suggestions to governments and other people responsible for protecting grasslands.

Research scientists put a radio transmitter into this rhino's horn so they can track its movements.

National Parks and reserves

National Parks and reserves around the world include areas, such as the Serengeti in Tanzania, where grasslands and their wildlife are protected by law. Park workers control who enters the **habitat**. They keep illegal hunters out by guarding animals or by patrolling areas. Tourists are encouraged to visit. The money they pay to get into parks is used to buy equipment and provide jobs, especially for local people. In Namibia, former hunters use their tracking skills to help tourists spot grassland wildlife.

Conservation groups

Conservation groups encourage people to give money and time to protect grasslands by making them aware of the problems grasslands face. For example, WWF Australia is helping landowners in Monaro, New South Wales, to control **grazing** and set up reserves in order to protect unusual grassland plants.

Wardens at the Virunga National Park in central Africa go on regular patrols to try and stop poachers from killing elephants for their ivory tusks.

Research a grassland food web

You can research your own grassland food chains and webs, using information from this and other books, TV programmes and the Internet. Work out which **organisms** live in a particular grassland. It helps to group them together – which are the insects, birds and **mammals**, for example? Then think about their lives:

1. How does the weather affect them?
2. How do they get their food, water or shelter?
3. What is their role in the grassland – **producer** or **consumer**, **predator** or **prey**?

To make a food chain, it may help to identify the biggest predator and then find out the different prey it eats, what the prey itself eats, and so on, until you get to a plant – the start of the food chain!

You might be able to visit a grassland habitat, like this North American National Park, to do your own research!

Where are the world's main grasslands?

This map shows the location of the major grassland **habitats** across the world.

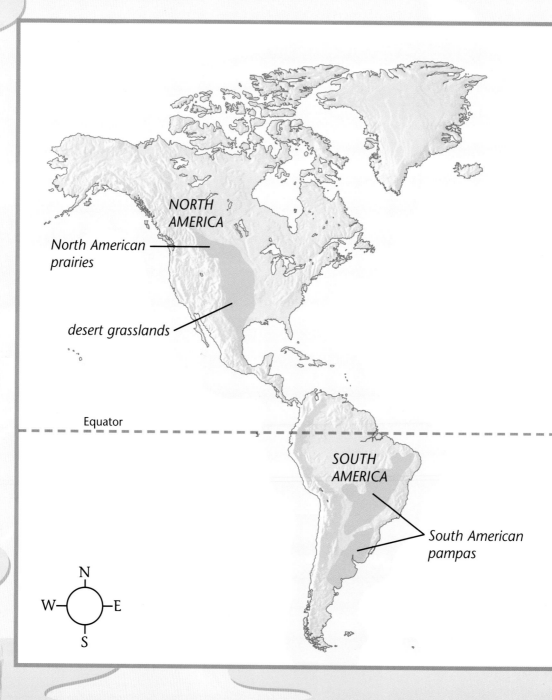

NORTH
AMERICA

North American
prairies

desert grasslands

Equator

SOUTH
AMERICA

South American
pampas

N
W—E
S

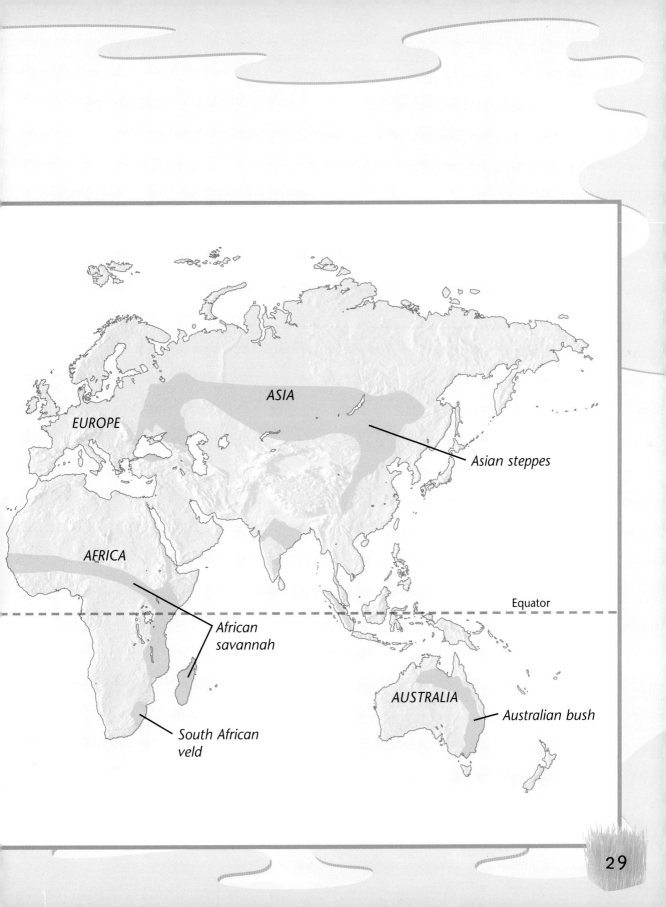

EUROPE

ASIA

Asian steppes

AFRICA

Equator

African savannah

AUSTRALIA

Australian bush

South African veld

Glossary

adapted having special features that help an organism live in its habitat

bacteria (singular bacterium) tiny living decomposers found everywhere

bird of prey bird that hunts animals for food

carnivore animal that eats the flesh of another animal

carrion dead and rotting animals

climate the general conditions of weather in an area

conservation protecting and saving the natural environment

consumers organisms that eat other organisms

decomposers organisms that break down and get nutrients from dead plants and animals and their waste

endangered when a species is at risk of dying out completely

energy power to grow, move and do things

excrete to get rid of bodily wastes

extinct when a species has died out completely

fungi group of decomposer organisms including mushrooms, toadstools and their relatives

graze to eat growing grass

habitat place where an organism lives

herbivore animal that eats plants

larvae (singular larva) the young of some insects and other animals

mammals group of animals that feed their babies on milk from their own bodies

native belonging naturally to an area

nectar sugary substance made by plants to attract insects, which eat it

nutrients chemicals that plants and animals need to live

omnivore animal that eats both plants and other animals

organism living thing

parasite organism that lives on or within another living thing and feeds from it, without offering any benefit in return

photosynthesis process by which plants make their own food using carbon dioxide (a gas in the air), water and energy from sunlight

pollination when pollen moves from the male part of a flower and enters the female part to form seeds

predators animals that hunt and eat other animals

prey animals that are caught and eaten by predators

primary consumers animals that eat plants

producer organism (plant) that can make its own food

rodents mammals with large gnawing front teeth, such as mice and rats

sap liquid in the stems and roots of a plant that it uses to transport food

scavengers organisms that feed on dead plants and animals and their waste

secondary consumers animals that eat primary consumers and other secondary consumers

species group of organisms that are very similar and can breed together to produce young

temperate belonging to a region of the world that has warm summers and cold, wet winters

tropical belonging to a region of the world that is warm all year round but has one or more rainy seasons

Find out more

Books and CD-Roms

Cycles in Nature: Food chains, Theresa Greenaway (Hodder Wayland/Raintree Steck-Vaughn, 2001)

Science Answers: Food Chains and Webs, Louise and Richard Spilsbury (Heinemann Library, 2004)

Taking Action: Friends of the Earth, Louise Spilsbury (Heinemann Library, 2000)

Food Chains and Webs CD-ROM (Heinemann Library, 2004) has supporting interactive activities and video clips.

Websites

These sites are about biomes of the world. Click on 'grasslands' to find out more about the grasslands of the world.

www.blueplanetbiomes.org/grasslands.htm

www.enchantedlearning.com/biomes/grassland/grasslands.html

This site also has many links to their conservation projects

www.panda.org/news_facts/education/virtual_wildlife/wild_places/grasslands.cfm

Find out more about the conservation work of these organizations at:

www.foe.co.uk   Friends of the Earth UK

www.foe.org.au   Friends of the Earth Australia

Index

Titles in the *Food Chains and Webs* series include:

Hardback   0 431 11903 1

Hardback   0 431 11905 8

Hardback   0 431 11904 X

Hardback   0 431 11902 3

Hardback   0 431 11901 5

Hardback   0 431 11900 7

Find out about the other titles in this series on our website www.heinemann.co.uk/library